From The Horse's Mouth
(Walking a mile in your horse's shoes)

By
Bob Kinford

www.2lazy4u.us

Cover Photo by Catie Kinford

Contents

Introduction

Everyone is always looking for that "magic bullet" to take care of all of the problems they have with their horses. The problem is, there is no silver bullet. After working with thousands of horses over the decades, three things have become clear to me.

First, every horse is an individual, and second, every horse is a product of its past. Third, two horses can have nearly identical pasts, yet hold opposite lessons from them. The best analogy I can come up with is two children raised by an alcoholic parent. One might grow up to repeat the life of its alcoholic parent—getting drunk, beating the kids and kicking the dog, while the other grows up to abhor alcohol and cannot raise a hand to their child under any circumstance.

This individuality makes working with each horse a unique experience. Developing a relationship with horses is much like developing relationships with people. While one might be willing, open, and easy to work with, the next could be from a past full of abuse is suspicious, angry, and looking for an opportunity to lash out. Yet another might have past injuries that cause problems due to pain or vision loss, and these problems can cause adverse reactions to what we are asking of it.

This brings to light the difficulty of describing just how to relate to your horse(s). Bill and Tom Dorrance started a revolution in training horses by using methods that allow your horses to relate to you in a way they can understand. However, many people have a hard time understanding the philosophy, and also the mechanics, behind things like timing, balance, and feel. Then there are also the misconceptions we naturally believe.

First, we must realize that we are NOT teaching the horse to do things it doesn't already know. Keep a horse penned up in a stall with no exercise for a couple of weeks and turn it out in the arena, chances are it's going to run hard, stop hard, roll back over its hindquarters and run off again. It will run in circles, changing direction and leads on its own. Watch horses in a pasture, and you'll see that they might back up a couple of steps, or even step sideways to give a horse higher on the pecking order a little more space. Horses that are pastured with cattle will chase them around or even get one in a pasture corner and hold them there, (like a cutting horse), just for fun. This brings us to the realization that rather than *teaching* the horse, we have to learn how to communicate with the horse. We have to be able to tell it what *we want it to do*, in a way that the horse will understand, as well as understand what the horse is telling us by its behaviors.

Secondly, we must realize that every time we handle a horse, we are training it. We are either doing things in a manner that allows the horse to communicate more easily, and be more willing. Or we are doing things that keep the horse at the same level, and making the horse resent us and become less willing to be our partner.

The vast differences between horses and their issues, and the vast differences people have in learning, makes writing a *how to* book on relating to and training horses seem to be a futile effort. It would be much simpler if the horses could just tell us with their own voices.

The goal of **From The Horse's Mouth** is to let the reader walk a mile (or two) in the horseshoes of their equine friends. Let them walk in the shoes of horses to learn why the problem lies not in the horse, but in owner's own deafness to what the horse might be telling them.

Dedicated to P.M. Rainstorm who was my favorite horse for 25 years. One quarter Saddlebred and three quarters Egyptian Arab, he was as far from being a cow-horse as you can get without changing species. Yet, if I had been paid a nickel per pound for every animal I roped to doctor off him, I would be a man rich in money. Instead I am rich in the memories of the miles he carried me on ranches and feedlots, and of all the cattle we handled together. When my life here is over, I expect to see him; ears up, eyes bright, and running to meet me at the pearly gates, ready to ride new range. He is the "interpreter" for *From The Horse's Mouth*. He is also the horse on the cover.

Stormy

As corny as it may sound, I actually *was* born on a dark and stormy night. That fact, combined with my mother's name of *Rainbow Girl* (and that our owner hadn't much of an imagination) I was dubbed with the moniker of *PM Rainstorm.*

The first couple of years were pretty boring. I was king of my realm, but the half acre lot in the middle of Albuquerque didn't give me much room to stretch my legs. Other than being forced behind a gate to be gelded at six months, and a couple of more times to be wormed, no one did anything with me other than feed me apples and pet me. Just before I turned two, they decided to put me in back of the gate for something, and I struck the vet on the shoulder and bit his helper. After a few heated words with our owner, the vet and his helper got into their truck and left. I had won...I really showed those two leggers what happens when you mess with me!

A couple of days later I was in my stall munching on hay when the two legger who put shoes on my mom showed up with a trailer. If his legs would have grown as much as his upper body he would have been six inches taller, so I had already dubbed him "No Legs."

He backed the trailer up to my stall and made an alley into the trailer. Then he came into my stall and scratched and rubbed me a few minutes, then moved my hay up to the front of the trailer. As he was having a cup of coffee and talking with my owner I started sniffing the trailer. I could smell other horses, and my breakfast was up in the front, so after a few minutes checking out the trailer, I stepped into it and started finishing my breakfast. The next thing I knew the trailer door closed and I was headed down the road. I started to panic, and screamed for my mother, but then my curiosity got the better of me. I began paying more attention to the traffic and scenery we were passing through.

Little did I realize that not only was my life changing, but also my attitude about cooperating with two leggers. Rather than being resentful at what 'ol No Legs was doing with me, I found myself curious and willing. Together we competed in Western Pleasure and Team Penning. I carried No Legs chasing the hounds in the Juan Thomas Hunt Club of New Mexico, jumping arroyos and fences, and picking up horses who had dropped their riders. We handled other horses and more cattle than I could count, in more conditions than I ever knew existed when I lived in that backyard.

Over the years, I watched No Legs work with a lot of horses. At times he was forced into using methods the horse owner wanted. Results from these methods were never what No Legs wanted, which is why he asked me to tell these two leggers what went wrong. The following are stories that some of these horses have dictated to me, so that their stories are told in their own words.

Flipper

I began as a broodmare prospect on a Nevada ranch. That way of life ended at the age of four when it was determined I was physically unable to have babies. It was then the two leggers decided to salvage me as a saddle horse. I was dubbed with the moniker "Flipper" by the first two legger who saddled me because I flipped over and broke his saddle. After I did the same thing to a second two legger's saddle, I was turned back out to pasture. I thought I showed them I wasn't to be messed with and figured they had learned their lesson.

A month later I was brought back into the pens and introduced to yet another two legger. Rather than just saddle me up as the other two leggers had done, this one started flipping a rope at me. I wasn't going to stand for any of this two legger nonsense. I tried running off, but the pen was too small and I couldn't get away. This two legger didn't get excited and just kept following me around and flipping the rope out at me. It didn't hit me every time he flipped it, and when it did, it didn't hurt. After a few minutes, I decided to stop and look at him, and when I did, he quit flipping the rope and stood there talking to me.

When he started to walk towards me I moved away and here came that flipping rope again. The two legger didn't seem excited or angry, he just kept moving towards me and flipping the rope at me,,and sometimes with it coming across my body. It didn't hurt, so after a while, I stopped again and faced him to see what he wanted.

This time when he came up to me, most of my fear of him was gone and I was beginning to be curious about what he wanted. What a surprise, all he seemed to want to do is scratch my neck and pet me!

Next he started rubbing me with the rope and casually flipping it over my body and dragging it off. This was a big difference from the other two leggers . All they had done was rope me, and fight with me to tie me up to a big post.. So far this one hadn't made a move to force me into anything.

He moved back once more and started flipping the rope at my hindquarters and moved at me in a sort of aggressive manner that told me I should move out, which I did. A couple of different times he flipped the rope in front of me and moved at my head, so I turned around and went the other way. While I moved in the directions he seemed to want, I was getting pretty tired of going back and forth, but he wasn't hurting me, so I kept doing what he asked. He was really getting my curiosity going. When he stood still again, I stopped and faced him...Just what *did* he want?

Next, he picked up a halter and lead rope and started to walk around me. Not wanting to lose sight of him, I turned so I could keep facing him. When he changed direction, I changed with him. Then he walked up to my head and began scratching me again while continuing to flip the lead rope over my body and neck. Once he flipped the rope over my neck, and rather than pulling it off, he began walking around me. Still curious (and not wanting him to chase me again) I followed him a few steps. He stopped and began scratching my neck and head, while talking to me. I didn't really know what was going on, but whatever was happening seemed to be making this two legger happy, which somehow made me feel at ease.

Once again he moved me out, and had me change directions a few times. I was beginning to enjoy this. When he took the pressure off of me this time, I faced him and took a couple of steps towards him. After rubbing my neck, face, and head for a few minutes, he put the halter on me. It had a rope attached, and when he put a little bit of pressure on the lead rope I panicked and ran backwards. Rather than trying to hold me, the two legger began chasing me backwards and working the rope in a way I couldn't get turned around to run off. Through all of this the two legger remained calm. After a few seconds he stopped chasing me backwards, and I stopped, too.

After rubbing me a few seconds, he started to walk around me, once again putting a little pressure on the rope. I went to backing up again, but not as fast as the first time. Sure enough he started chasing me backwards again. This time I decided to stop on my own. What was the point of running from him? He wasn't doing anything to hurt me and there was nothing in his attitude to make me afraid.

This time when he started to walk around me, and put a little pressure on the lead rope, I took a couple of steps forward. He stopped to rub my neck and face again. From the tone of his voice, it sure seemed like he was happy with me. Within a few more minutes I figured out that when there was pressure on the lead, all I had to do was step forward and the pressure went away. All I had to do was follow this two legger and there was no pressure.

Next he started flipping the longer rope over me again. I was used to this so I just stood there. Then he flipped it around my body and grabbed the end. Running the end through the hondo, he pulled it tight around my girth.

I began to rear up in a hurry, wanting that feeling to end, but before I got all the way up, the pressure disappeared. Once again the two legger let me relax and scratched my neck a bit. He pulled the rope around my girth tight and once again when I started to rear the pressure disappeared, so I came back to the ground. As soon as I was on the ground, he tightened the rope again, and then released it as soon as I started up. Within a few minutes of this, I realized the pressure wasn't hurting me so I quit trying to rear up. Sure enough, he went to rubbing and scratching my neck again.

He kept adding more pressure and releasing it until

my reaction was to step into the pressure rather than try to pull away from it. Next, he did the same thing on my feet. Once I gave to the pressure on my feet, he once again applied pressure to my girth. When I gave to the pressure, he rubbed and scratched my neck, then let me go back to my pen.

The next day we repeated all of this. This time I just gave to the pressure rather than fight it. As I was not fighting the pressure, he put a saddle on me and tightened it up, but not real tight. After leading me around a bit, I got used to the constant pressure while walking; then he tightened it up a little more. By this time I was used to the pressure and was relaxed. In fact, I was curious to find out what this two legger would want to do next. Within a few days he was riding me out in the pastures, and to my surprise, I actually enjoyed it!

Miss Flash

I was purchased as a long yearling by a race horse syndicate as a futurity prospect. Having paid $35,000 for me, the partners had high hopes for my career as a racehorse.

At the time I had no experience with two leggers other than being herded from one place to the next, or into a trailer. When it came time to begin training, I was cornered in my stall while a tall two legger put a halter with a rope on it on me. Then the stall door was opened and I was taken down the breezeway of the barn, then down the alley to the round corral. I had no idea I was supposed to follow the two legger holding the rope, so I pulled back and he jerked on me while a sawed off two legger following me would shake his head and tap my rump with a soft rope until I went forward.

Once in the round corral, the one leading me hobbled me, put a saddle on my back, a snaffle bit in my mouth, and turned me loose...or so I thought. I turned and started bucking towards the outside of the pen, and when I was halfway there, I felt a sharp pain across my nose as the two legger jerked on the line. This two legger kept jerking on me until I finally stopped moving. Then he flipped the end of the lunge line at me again and I started running and bucking. He kept jerking on me until I slowed down and quit bucking.

I didn't slow down or stop bucking because of what he was doing, it was because I was getting tired. He jerked me around and started me in the other direction. I tried bucking a little bit, and running off, but every time I tried, this tall two legger kept jerking on that nose chain. When the tall two legger decided he had enough accomplished for the day, he unsaddled me and called for the short two legger. The two of them repeated the procedure they had in bringing me to the round corral. This time I wanted to run off and get back to my stall. That tall two legger kept jerking on my nose when I tried to pass him up, so it was a *big* relief when I was finally back home.

By the end of the third day I resigned myself to the fact I had to follow the tall two legger to the torture chamber. I also resigned myself to the fact I had to wear the saddle, even though I was still giving a few jumps to try and get it off.

On the fourth morning, once I was saddled, the short two legger was called in and told to get on me. The two leggers had a short argument about whether or not I was ready to ride. The sawed off two legger didn't think I was ready, and was against having the taller one keep me under control with the lunge line. Finally the short two legger complied, put a foot in the stirrup and swung on top of me.

As soon as he hit the saddle I jumped up, turned, and went to bucking as hard as I could. The two legger on top of me was being as calm and quiet as he could, while the one on the ground kept jerking on the lunge line. I managed to get a couple of turns and the jerking on my nose stopped.

About that time the two legger on the ground started hollering "BAIL OFF!"

The two legger on top of me hollered back "I can't! My foot is tied to the stirrup!"

With that the two legger on the ground dropped the lunge line and the two legger on top of me started gently pulling my nose around until I started circling and finally came to a stop. Once I was stopped, the two legger on the ground came over and untied the knot which had formed around No Leg's leg and the stirrup.

After a short argument, the sawed off two legger on my back convinced the taller one to get out of the round corral or he would quit. No Legs was starting eight of us, and four others bucked at least as hard as I did. Despite getting bucked off fourteen to eighteen times a day, he still won out.

A few days later he had the other seven   settled down and loping in both directions. I had something hurting in my left hind pastern when I tried to lope to the left which was why I was bucking. Once again the two leggers got to arguing, with No Legs telling the boss I had something wrong with my back left leg. The boss watched as No Legs tried getting me to lope to the left. After a few minutes he told No Legs there was nothing wrong with me, and to keep going until I loped to the left on the correct lead.

No Legs kept going that day until I finally gave in and loped a couple of times around the round corral to the left. When No Legs came to my stall the next day, my back left pastern was swollen and I could not put any weight on it.

No Legs called his boss over and showed him my leg. After that I saw him throw his saddle into the back of his pickup, and I never saw him again.

X-rays showed I had had a couple of bone spurs. If they would have been discovered before they broke off, I would have had a racing career. As it was I went from race prospect to broodmare in a flash. If the two leggers would have let me understand what they wanted instead of forcing the issue, perhaps I wouldn't have bucked so hard the spurs broke off. If the boss would have listened to No Legs, they could have found the problem and I'd still have a racing career.

Shelly

I really like people. My first memories are of kids playing with me. I loved it when whey would come out to the pasture and play with me. They would crawl around underneath me and swing on my tail. One day, one of them just crawled on me with a halter and started riding me around. We never did much, just went around on the trails at my own pace. I absolutely *loved it!*

When I was four my two legger family had to move and could not take me with them. They gave me to a really nice woman. She wanted me to do things like slide stops, roll backs, spins and lead changes. It sounded like it would be fun, but as soon as she started to lope me to the right, it hurt so badly I wouldn't pick up the lead. The harder she tried to get me to pick up that right lead, the more it hurt; it got to the point I was frustrated and gave a couple of jumps. My new two legger fell off. I hadn't mean to make her fall, so I went back to see if she was OK.

She was a little shaken, but unhurt. For my next ride, she took me to another two legger who specialized in training horses. This two legger warmed me up to the left, and I was just fine. Then she started trying to make me lope to the right, and the pain started again. She also kept pushing until the pain got so bad I had to jump away from her. When she got up she told my new two legger I was dangerous and that she should get rid of me.

Luckily this new two legger had faith in me. A couple of weeks later she loaded me in the trailer. After several hours we finally stopped and I was introduced to No Legs. He saddled me up and took me to the arena. When he started trotting to the right he made a comment that my way of traveling in that direction felt odd to him. Then he asked me to lope
going to the right. He mentioned that it felt like I had no idea of how of how to travel that direction. Before my two legger left, No Legs told her he would take it easy on me and would

try to figure out why I was so stiff and rough going right.

The next few weeks were interesting. No Legs rode me every day. He never really pushed the issue of loping to the right, but was doing exercises to limber up my body with lateral movement. No matter what he did, my movement to the right did not improve. Every day when he unsaddled me he poked and prodded my right side. Then he would pick up my back right leg and stretch it out then pull it forward, leading me at a trot each time to see if it made a difference in the way I traveled.

Then one day he put a postage-stamp saddle on me. When he started to trot me to the right he exclaimed "That's it!" and reached down and started feeling the top of my back right rib. I wasn't even sure when I had injured that rib.

No Legs and my two legger took me to a chiropractor a few days later. He confirmed what No Leg had thought. After three treatments all of my stiffness was gone. Before long I was able to do all of the things my two legger wanted me to do.

Occasionally I need to go back for a follow up, but other than that I'm now enjoying being ridden by my two legger no matter what we are doing.

Barney

They call me Barney...Barney the Bronc. All of the cowboys who had ridden me on the old UL-C wanted me to take a trip to France, in many containers. They all knew that sometime during the day I was going to uncork on them. It wasn't that I bucked that hard, but once I got started it seemed to them as if I just wouldn't stop. It was the opinion of these two leggers that I liked to buck, and that there was no way to predict when I would decide to break in two. It got to the point where the manager was planning on selling me. While I was waiting for the next horse sale to come up I was put out to pasture to fatten up a bit.

Then came the day I was accidentally ridden by a two legger the other horses on the ranch referred to as No Legs. Now you are probably wondering how a person could accidentally ride a horse.

On the day of this ride, No Legs and half the crew had to move the bull calf pairs about ten miles to a different pasture. The cattle were half spoiled so it was going to be one of those long days where the two leggers would need to change horses. One of the two leggers, named Stanley, was responsible for meeting up with the rest of the crew in the early afternoon with fresh horses. Well, Stanley had a typical sense of humor for this particular bunch of two leggers. When he caught up the fresh horses, rather than catch one of the other broke horses in No Leg's string, he caught me. I'd planted Stanley like dry-land wheat two times in one day the last time he'd ridden me. No Legs had given him a bad time for falling off a horse that couldn't buck as hard as the horse plugged into the front of a Wal Mart®, so this was to be his payback.

When we met up with the crew, No Legs unsaddled Storms and threw his wood on me. "Hey Stanley, glad you brought me a good broke horse out of my string!"

Grinning from ear to ear Stanley replied "Just want to make sure you have a good ride No Legs!"

No Legs threw a leg over me and we trotted over to the cattle. About ten minutes later we were headed down into a draw and I stumbled. No Legs picked up on the reins a bit to steady me and I started squalling and bucking.

After four or five jumps he quit trying to pull my head up with the bridle.   In the next half hour I went to bucking with him three times. All three times he wound up stopping me by pulling up on the get down rope.

For those of you who are not familiar with the term, those who ride in the buckaroo, or vaquero tradition, will often have a light ¼" bosal as well as the bit. This bosal can be used in some stages of training when a horse is being transitioned into the bridle. When not being used as a mecate rein, it is used to lead the horse rather than by the rein, and is referred to as "get down" rope.

After No Legs got me to quit bucking the third time, he stepped off and removed his bridle. Then he brought his get down rope around my neck to make a set of mecate reins and stepped back on.

Finally someone had figured me out! I wasn't really a bad horse, but my teeth had some pretty good hooks on them. They didn't bother me most of the time, but I never held a bit that well to begin with. When my teeth were bothering me I never held onto it, and just a light tap with the bit would hurt like heck. After getting my teeth floated I spent several years at the old UL-C.

Sis

I was one of those "backyard" horses. I could be haltered and led around a bit, but basically had no manners. I did like the two leggers, especially the kids, but no one ever asked anything of me so I didn't learn much. Then one night the head two legger ran out of money in a poker game, bet me in place of cash and lost.

The two legger who now owned me wanted to sell me, but as I didn't know anything, he sent me to a woman to start me under saddle. He only gave her ten days to do the job, so you might say I had a rough start. Rather than start me out in a non-leverage snaffle or hackamore, she started me out in a broken mouthed shanked bit. Needless to say I didn't have much handle or stop, but I didn't buck or run off so I was considered green broke.

It didn't take long for the new owner to find a buyer. My new two legger was a little girl with no fear and a need for speed. It all started out innocently enough. She wanted to see how fast I could run. We went to flying across the desert, leaping gullies and sage brush. I didn't need to know how to stop as she wanted to run for as long as I wanted to. Then she started racing me against other horses. Before long she had me trained to grab the bit and start running. Sometimes I would just trot, but walking was *not* an option.

Her parents were getting worried that I was going to hurt her, so they sold me to a couple of horse trainers. They put me in a double twisted wire snaffle and a German Martingale to try and get me slowed down. After a month of jerking and sawing on my mouth with that contraption they still couldn't get me to go slower than a trot. Heaven forbid if they ever made the mistake of giving me a bit of room because I would take that inch and run for several miles.

Then one day they went out to the desert to put some miles on a few the horses they were training and had a couple of friends tag along. One of them was No Legs. Now he had heard about what a handful I was, and had heard about my history. At the end of the ride I was fairly mad, and, (as usual), my mouth was bleeding from all the sawing that was being done on it with that twisted wire snaffle. By the time we got home, No Legs had bought me.

The next day he saddled me up, but instead of putting a bit in my mouth, he put a hackamore on my head. Everyone was telling him he was crazy, that if anything I needed a bigger bit to get me to slow down. He ignored them, pulled my head around to the side and stepped up into the saddle.

I started to do my usual run off, but all I could do was go in a tight circle. When I slowed down, he let me go straight a few steps. Within a few steps I would start to run off and he would catch me in mid stride and circle me around again until I'd slow down. About the third or fourth time I figured out he was going the same direction and started to pull back against him, but instead, he pulled me in the direction I was pulling towards. I also realized I didn't have any pain in my mouth.

It seemed that the first couple of rides we were just going in circles without getting anywhere. At times he would circle me really tight, and then start asking me to back. Since I wasn't fighting the pain in my mouth, I started to understand how to give to pressure rather than fight it. Within a week, I was calming down and beginning to understand that it was OK to walk.

For a month (maybe more) everything we did was at a walk or trot. He did a lot of stopping and backing, but he was doing that a bit different too. First, he only asked me at a walk. He would tell me "whoa," and then it felt as if all of the motion went out of his body. His hands would lower until they touched my neck, then he would repeat "WHOA" in a more stern voice and pick up on the reins until I started backing. After a few days I figured out that when he said "Whoa," and I stopped, he would reach down and pat my neck rather than pull on the reins.

Within a few days I was always stopping at a walk, so he started stopping me at a trot. Within a few days I was stopping the instant he told me "whoa" without being pulled on.

Then came the real test...loping and stopping. Now I have to admit, it did cross my mind to go running off. However, I was also beginning to like this stopping thing. It was fun to see just how fast I could stop when No Legs wanted me to.

We headed out to the desert and trotted for several miles non-stop before he asked me to lope. By now I was warmed up, relaxed, and paying attention to what he wanted me to do. When I transitioned into the lope I was relaxed and didn't want to run at full speed.

After several miles I was feeling good and suddenly he told me "whoa" and relaxed his body. Knowing he wanted me to stop and began to slow down, then he said "whoa" one more time and picked up on the reins. He timed picking up on the reins as I was reaching underneath myself with my back legs. I stopped so fast it surprised me! No Legs reached down, patted my neck and praised me.

While I shouldn't have been, I was surprised at how much fun it was to stop hard. Duh...My favorite thing to do when I was playing in my pen was to run as hard as I could, stop and change direction.

By taking away the pain, teaching me to give to pressure, and by timing his cues (and balance) in a way I could understand, No Legs turned me into a willing partner for whatever he wanted to do. I was not only willing, but looked forward to our rides and anticipating what he wanted next.

Rodney

If it wasn't for bad luck, I'd have no luck at all. I was bred to be a cutting horse. As a yearling, it was fun running around a pasture with other horses, but I managed to get a cactus thorn stuck in my right eye. Luckily it was discovered and removed before an infection set in, but after that, I couldn't really see well out of it.

One day when the two leggers brought a bunch of cows into the pens to work, I just happened to come in with them. But, because they thought I was in the way, one of the two leggers tied me to a T-post.

The next thing I knew there was a blur coming at me from my right side. I tried to get out of the way and hung the corner of my jaw on the T-post, slashing my throat clear to the point of my other jaw. Pulling backwards, I manage to skin my lower jaw clear to the end of my chin, with the whole thing hanging there like some sort of macabre bloody beard.

The two leggers managed to get everything sewed back up. Unfortunately, while I was healing up, I didn't see the rattlesnake to the right of where I was grazing. This one didn't rattle to warn me, it just up and bit me on the right front leg. Like I say, if it wasn't for bad luck, I wouldn't have any luck at all!

Then one day my two legger put me in a trailer and hauled me over to No Legs to get me started under saddle. He told him about the wreck with the T-post, and the snakebite incident, but he had forgotten about the thorn in my eye.

No Legs started out desensitizing me, taking care to work a little harder on my right side. He even worked at getting me to give to pressure. He could lunge me with a rope around any of my feet, and I would stop when he put pressure on the rope. I would even follow the pressure and walk up to him. He could even lead me around with just a rope around my body.

He saddled me and drove me for a week. I was doing everything he asked. I could slide stop when he asked. I was picking up my leads, turning whenever he wanted, and doing everything right. He could put his foot in the stirrup, stand up and pet me up and down both sides. I was even having fun doing it.

As he was unsaddling me one day, he was praising me and talking about how he was going to ride me the next day. He nonchalantly unhooked the breast collar and flipped it under my throat and over my neck.

I didn't recognize the breast collar as it came up, and flashed back to the snake. I started to jump out of the way and forgot the saddle was on me. Feeling the pressure from the cinch, I jumped to get away from it. Five jumps later, I ran into the fence and stopped, but was still shaken. No Legs hadn't a clue of my vision problem, but decided that I needed more desensitizing; he knew he wasn't enough of a bronc rider to last through one of my storms.

The next day, I was still shaken, which made it hard for him to catch me. Once he caught me and started brushing me I settled down. He sacked me out with ropes and a blanket. He saddled me and drove me. I was doing everything just fine and he decided to give me a break. Just then a dust devil came into the pen and I broke in two, my feet nearly six feet off the ground. Once again I bucked until I hit the fence, then stood there shaking.

No Legs was really confused at this point. Nothing he could do would make me spook, let alone buck. It was some unseen cue that would set me off to making the NFR bucking horse of the year look like something plugged into the front of a Wal Mart® store.

Now, he already knew that the cattle had been run at me from my right side when I cut my throat, and that the snake had bitten me on my right side. He was assuming that the memories of my past traumas that he was aware of had triggered my bucking, but couldn't understand what was really setting me off.

The next thing he did was turn me into the "Incredible Plastic Horse." He put an old saddle on me and sacked me out with a plastic garbage bag. I didn't mind him doing that, so I just stood there. Next he hung plastic trash cans (some of them containing several aluminum cans) all over the saddle. He also hung a couple off my halter. Through all of this I stood still. Heck, I *knew* where he was at all times and I *knew* that nothing he was doing was hurting me.

Then he started lunging me. The bags rattled a bit, but I knew they were there, so I knew there was nothing to blow up about. He then put the lines on me and drove me. I stopped, turned, and did whatever he asked without blowing up.

When No Legs was done working me, he gave me a drink, loosened my cinch a bit and tied me up. Sure enough, about a half an hour later a slight breeze blew up a little cloud of dust, and I hit the fan. I pulled back and bucked in place for who knows how long until I settled down.

To No Legs, I was a real quandary. I knew why I was getting spooked, but there was no way I could explain it to him. There was one more trauma I had suffered that my two legger had forgotten to tell No Legs. It was OK though, because in spite of his lack of information, No Legs was teaching me that bucking did no good.

He did not realize that my problem lay not just in the fact I had cut my throat and had been bitten by a rattlesnake. The problem was in the fact that I couldn't see well out of my right eye. After being worked with the plastic bags tied to me every day (and wearing them a few hours after) I learned that bucking did not do me any good.

No Legs finally went to riding me, but just wasn't satisfied with my progress. Whenever we would come to something on my right side I didn't recognize I'd turn my head to the right and start drifting to the left. He was beginning to wonder if I could see out of my right eye.

Then my two legger showed up one day, and told No Legs that he had remembered about the cactus thorn that had been stuck in my right eye. After discussing it, they both agreed I would never make a very good ranch horse. I would be almost useless in a pen of cattle as I would never really be able to recognize what was going on to my right. The roads on my two legger's ranch are so rough that on many of them you can't go faster than a horse can walk. My job description was changing from cutting horse to wagon horse.

No Legs rounded up some harness and a single tree. After driving me in the harness with the rattling chains for a few days, he hooked me up to a single tree attached to a couple of tires.

After a couple of weeks dragging the tires, I graduated to pulling a small wagon. This was more like it. Because I was wearing blinders, I could travel without being distracted by those pesky shadows to my right.

Thanks to the fact that No Legs and my own two legger figured out my vision problem, I now have a job I'm not only comfortable with, but that I actually enjoy.

Chief

When I first met No Legs, I was working in a dude string. He would show up once a week and replace the shoes on those of us who needed it. He liked me right off the bat because I was not only gentle to shoe, but because I would never lean on him while he was shoeing me.

After I had been there a few months a couple of two leggers showed up looking for a horse. Being as I was a dark bay with a blanket as white as new fallen snow, and sorrel spots, I stuck out like a diamond in a coal mine. After a few test rides they bought me and took me home.

Things went really well for a few months. The two legger who rode me was an FBI agent so he would sometimes be gone for a few weeks between rides. This was a heck of a lot easier than working in that dude string. I didn't want to wind up back there so I took really good care of him.

Then one windy spring day he decided to saddle me up and go for a ride with his wife. We were almost home when a big blue tarp came out of a dry irrigation ditch. It wrapped around my legs and part of it flew over the top of me. It was then I sensed my two legger was afraid. He was also swinging his arms back and forth trying to get the tarp off his head. As a result, he pulled me off balance and I stepped off the edge of the ditch. After rolling several times I was at the bottom of the ditch while my two legger was lying half way up the ditch. Being a little spooked about the whole thing, (especially since my two legger was hollering and screaming at me), I ran home.

He didn't try riding me for a few days. When he started to get on me, I sensed that he was nervous about something. Every time we rode past anything that might blow in the air or might move if I stepped on it, he would tense up. I didn't know why he was so tense and nervous, but if he was, then I needed to be on the lookout as well! Within a few weeks he was so nervous I was ready to jump out of my skin every time he took me for a ride. Then came the day when I actually did step on a stick. He was so scared his whole body jumped in the saddle. Of course his fear went through me, so I jumped as well, which resulted in my two legger falling to the ground.

This time I just stood there, but rather than get on me, he led me home. The next day I was loaded into the trailer. To my surprise, rather than being returned to the dude string or taken to a sale barn, I was unloaded at a training stables. Adding to my surprise, No Legs came out to get me.

As soon as my two legger left, No Legs saddled me up and took me to the arena. I didn't sense any fear from him so I just stood perfectly still when he got on my back. He walked me a bit, and then started trotting me. It was nice to be able to relax for a change rather than being tensed up and wondering what my two legger was so afraid of.

After a couple of times around the arena, he called out to a two legger to get a towel and throw it to him as we went by. No Legs was still relaxed so I had no reason to be afraid as the towel was thrown to him. I kept going straight as he swung the towel around my head, and even drug it across the top of my head. Next he took me out for a ride on the trails, and even along a road. I never took a wrong step. It was such a relief to not be constantly worrying about why my rider was filled with so much fear.

That evening my two legger showed up with his saddle. He was telling No Legs how surprised he was that he was able to "fix" me in such short order.

My two legger was nervous as he saddled me up. As he started to mount me, he was so scared he was shaking, so I was fidgety as well and stepped away from him.

Seeing this, No Legs suggested that he ride me first. No Legs didn't get his moniker from being long legged. The stirrups were set about six inches too long for him so he was wallering around all over the place trying to get his leg over the top of the saddle. Of course he wasn't worried about anything so I just stood there perfectly still.

Once on top of me he told my two legger to throw me the towel he had placed on the fence. My two legger immediately refused, claiming he didn't want to get No Legs "bucked off." After arguing about it for a couple of minutes, he called out the two legger who had thrown him the towel that morning. No Legs started trotting in circles and playing towel catch with the two legger.

After No Legs explained to my two legger that I was acting the way I was because HE was afraid, he began thinking about it. No Legs got him on top of me and started playing towel catch. Within a few minutes my two legger was relaxed, and so was I. It had been impossible for me to relax when My two legger was so worried about me spooking. I had no idea what he *was* worried about, but as soon as he quit worrying and started relaxing, it was sure nice to be able to be able to relax and enjoy the trails again!

Gertrude

The only problem I really had was my two legger. He had absolutely no sense of timing, balance, feel, or focus. As a result I had no clue as to what he wanted. This was especially true when he wanted me to stop because he kept leaning forward, which told me to go faster. He also kept leaning to the side and falling off.

Then one day he and his wife decided to go to a clinic on speed control and stopping. What a mess. He couldn't get me to go into a trot without falling off, let alone go into a lope and stop. At the end of the clinic they talked to No Legs about taking lessons on a family plan.

A few days later they loaded the kids and all of us horses into the trailer and headed over to No Legs for their first lesson. He already had his horse, Storms, saddled and warmed up. Just a few minutes into this first lesson he stopped everything and had my two legger take my saddle and bridle off, put my halter on, and then get on me bareback.

Needless to say, my two legger didn't feel comfortable with the idea. No Legs told him that he needed to develop balance to stay on me, and that he needed to be able to feel what I was doing in order to do that.

While No Legs led me off at a walk, he told my two legger to close his eyes and tell him when my right front foot was leaving the ground. At first he let my two legger hold onto my mane for security. After several weeks of lessons, (and practicing at home), my two legger could finally feel what my feet were doing at a walk. Next we practiced at a trot. By the time my two legger could feel where my feet were at a trot, he also had the balance to stay in the middle of me without falling forward or sliding off the side of me.

Next we started working on getting my two legger to balance himself in a way that would communicate to me what he wanting me to do. No Legs really concentrated on teaching my two legger to get me to relax and give to pressure, which was something I had never learned.

The whole goal of these lessons was to get the family, especially my two legger, confident enough in their riding so that they could take horse camping trips into the desert. After several months of twice a week lessons, No Legs began meeting us in the desert to conduct the lessons in the environment the family wanted to ride in.

On the last ride we took with No Legs my two legger was confident enough in himself, and me, that he put the reins on my neck so he could light a cigarette. We were just coming to the bottom of a fairly steep hill at the time. I stumbled and dropped my head then started trotting off. The reins had dropped over my head, but my two legger had gained enough balance and focus that he didn't panic. He simply said "whoa," reached down, grabbed both sides of my breast collar, and pulled up on it. Since we had been working together on the giving to pressure, and he remained balanced, I simply stopped.

Since then we have spent many enjoyable weekends exploring the desert, and he hasn't fallen off once.

Ahab

My start in life was great. My owners imprinted me at birth. By the time I was four months old I was getting my feet trimmed, wormed and vaccinated with no problem. I enjoyed being around people and doing things with them. Then at three years old I was sent out to be started under saddle.

The person to saddle me the first time was nice, but, as they say, "young and dumb." Since I was gentle, he just threw the saddle on me and cinched it up tight without preparing me for the pressure. When I started to walk, the pressure from the cinch startled me and I began to buck, and eventually fell over backwards. I felt something in my withers but did not have any way to tell anyone about it. After ten days of cinching me up tight and having me buck, this young two legger told my owner that I was "too rank to ride."

My owner took me to No Legs and explained the situation as she saw it. He started out slow, doing his ground work and thought I was a pretty responsive and willing horse. He even put a rope around my girth and had me leading by that rope. When he saddled me, he didn't cinch it too tight, and I was comfortable enough to work without pain.

Then came the day for my first time under him. We walked around the round corral a few times in each direction with no problem. Then we started trotting. I was a little uncomfortable, but not too bad.

Then a sack blew up against the side of the round corral and I started to shy away from it. That is when the pain hit, and I started to buck, and buck hard! After several wild trips around the pen I lost my balance and fell on my belly and laid there. After a couple of minutes of sitting on me and waiting for me to get up, No Legs stepped off of me. With his weight off of me, I stood up.

Now he put together the fact that my bucking started when the sack had blown up against the round corral. He had no way of knowing that it wasn't the sack that made me start bucking, but the pain in my withers from flinching at the sack. All he could think was that I needed more sacking out.

He not only sacked me out in the round corral, but tied garbage bags and tin cans on my saddle and ponied me for hours in the desert, No Legs riding Storms. Every once in a while I would feel the pinch and go to bucking. It just didn't make any sense to either No Legs or my two legger. After several weeks I wasn't bucking quite as hard. In fact, I learned to just stop when it hurt. That was a new problem to solve, but No Legs figured I was safe enough to ride.

Now while No Legs was trying to get me safe to ride, my two legger was doing research to find a reason for my behavior. After all, I was a *gentle* horse who liked two leggers. There had to be a reason for what I was doing.

Then came the day of our defining wreck. We were heading across the desert at a trot when suddenly I stopped and picked my head up to look at some mustangs in the desert. No Legs just sat there expecting me to start bucking, but hoping I'd relax. Instead I threw myself down on my side.   The first thing to hit was his shoulder, then his head. After sliding on top of him a couple of feet I got up and ran home.

Luckily one of the neighbors happened to see the wreck and drove over to give No Legs a ride home. When he caught me, he noticed my eyes were bulging out like that two legger Rodney Dangerfield. He had never seen that in a horse, making it his first clue that I had something physically wrong. No Legs thought perhaps the bucking and throwing myself to the ground was a reaction to pain. I was making progress and learning, there just was no telling when the pain would strike, forcing me to buck or throw myself down.

About the time No Legs was completing the last week of his contract to ride me, my two legger discovered I probably had a pinched nerve in my withers from the first time I went over backwards. After taking me home, I was given two chiropractic/acupuncture treatments and my problem was solved. I was given to a young female two legger who loves to endurance ride. Three months after being given my treatments, I finished the Tevis cup in the top twenty. If anyone had properly diagnosed me at the start, both No Legs and I would have had an easier time of things.

Rudolph

No, I didn't have a red nose, but I did play a reindeer once...more or less.

It was on the ranch I had been born on, where I lived a fairly carefree life. Every once in a while the two legger kids would find some games to play with me. I wasn't old enough to be working under saddle. so their "games" usually consisted of petting me, crawling around underneath me and hanging off my neck or tail. I'd been raised with these two legged rug rats and enjoyed their attention.

Then one day, just before Christmas they came up with a new game. Deciding to play Santa and his elves, they decided I would make a good reindeer to pull their sleigh.

The sleigh consisted of an old toboggan. They fashioned a harness out of baling twine. Taking a bridle out of the tack room they put it on me, then tied a bunch more baling twine to the end of the reins to make them long enough to reach back to Santa's sleigh. Just in case I needed a little help in moving out, they tied a tire to the front of the sleigh so that they could throw it at my back legs, and be able to keep it if they needed it again. Like I say, these two legged rug rats were young and dumb.

Sadly enough, I was as young and dumb as my two leggers. Trusting them and not having a clue as to what their plans were, I stood there patiently enjoying their attention. That didn't last long though!

The next thing I know all three of them were on the sleigh in back of me yelling at me to "Giddy-up." I didn't really know what they wanted, but then suddenly something (the tire) hit me in the back legs. I gave a bit of a jump, not much, and the next thing I knew there was a jerk on my mouth and the sleigh ran into the back of me.

Suddenly my calmness was replaced by sheer, blind, panic. The two legger holding on to my baling twine lines wouldn't (or couldn't) let go. He was tearing into my mouth with the bridle, while the sleigh and tire kept banging into my legs. As I turned to go out the gate, the little two legger

slid into the fence and finally let go of the lines. No matter what I did, no matter how fast I went the sleigh and tire kept chasing me, and occasionally hitting me. Seeing the other horses across the fence, I made a beeline for them. I cleared the fence, but the tire and sleigh hung up, slamming me to the ground as my baling twine harness broke. I was scraped up a little bit, but not badly hurt.

However, I no longer trusted the two leggers. As long as they were in front of me and I could see them it wasn't bad. But I would no longer allow the two legged rug rats brush me, or for that matter, even get close to me. It wasn't long until the family decided I was too dangerous to have around and sold me.

Because I would kick at anyone going past my hind end, I was run loose into the trailer and hauled off to my new home. They backed the trailer into a hundred foot by hundred foot pen and turned me out.

My new two leggers bought me for two reasons. The first was because I was "cheap" and the second reason was they wanted a horse they "could learn with." My previous two leggers didn't tell them about my kicking or about my experience of playing one of Santa's reindeer. All they knew was that I was at the right age to be started under saddle.

These new two leggers did manage to catch me by feeding me some grain, but it took them several tries over a few days to do it. They tied me to a post and started trying to brush me. They started at my neck and worked their way back, but when they reached my back I got fidgety and started trying to turn and face them. The male two legger was so big he resembled a grizzly bear. He decided he would slam himself into the side of me and hold me to the fence. The next thing he knew he was lying on the ground and I was pulling back so hard I broke the lead rope. It just took a few more sessions before they were both bruised, battered and knew they were in over their heads. Besides that, I wasn't about to let them catch me so Grizzman could try manhandling me again.

A few days later a sawed off two legger showed up. After talking with my two leggers he came into my pen. He spent a few minutes working me around the pen, but he was doing things differently. When I felt pressured and started to run off, he would quit pressuring me. He kept working with me in a diagonal so that I kept getting closer to one of the corners. Before I knew it I was I a corner with nowhere to go but over the top of him.

While I stood there shaking and trying to figure out how to get out of the corner, he took a couple of steps back and just stood there calmly. I took that as my chance and tried to run past him, but he ran backwards at an angle, cutting me off, so I stopped and ran the other way. He managed to get me turned a couple of times before I blasted by him firing a kick at his head as I went.

This didn't seem to faze him. He just kept working me until he got me in a corner again. This time, once he got me to stop, he just turned around and left. It was a relief to be left alone. I just couldn't trust these two leggers a bit!

He showed up again the next day. This time he brought a saddle, blanket and some ropes into the pen with him. Once again he started working me diagonally across the pen until I was in a corner. When I started to run past him, he would flip the rope out in front of me and I'd turn back to the corner. After a few attempts I built up the courage to run into, and through the rope. He didn't get excited, he just kept working me across the pen to another corner.

I was a little calmer and thought I had him figured out. I really shouldn't have thought at all. When I ran by him this time, he flipped the rope at me and I didn't manage to run past it. Instead the rope tightened around my neck, then went slack. I ran around the pen kicking at the rope. After a couple of laps I realized that he was just standing there watching me run around. I also realized that I wasn't being hurt, so I stopped.

The two legger picked up the end of the rope and started coming up to me, coiling the rope as he came. Stupid two legger. I had more pen than he had rope so there was no way he was going to be able to hole me! I took off at a run, knowing he would wind up tripping, falling down and letting go of the rope. That was the one thing I learned well with Grizzman.

No Legs may have only been half the size of Grizzman, but he didn't trip and let go of the rope. Instead, as I ran off he threw himself to the ground and hung onto the rope. I didn't drag him far before I started getting short winded, so I stopped and turned to face him...and could breathe again.

No Legs stood up, brushed himself off, and started coming up the rope again just as if nothing had happened. I took off again and he just sat down like he was sliding into third base without letting go of the rope. Once again the rope came tight and it was getting hard to breathe.

This time when I stopped and faced him he was laughing. This was a switch. Everyone else had been panicking and yelling at me. This one was acting like it was some sort of game!

I tried running off a few more times, but the results didn't change. He just consistently sat down and let me drag him until I it was hard to breathe. Finally I decided it would be easier to let him come up the rope to see what he wanted.

When he got up to me, he just started rubbing my head and scratching me in back of my ears, the whole time talking to me in a soothing voice. Maybe this wasn't going to be so bad after all. He led me over to the saddle, picked up a halter with a long lead rope and put it on me. Next he removed the rope from around my neck.

He took that long lead and started flipping it up over my body. I had a flashback to my sleigh-pulling incident and panicked. I tried to run off, but he managed to keep pulling me around with the lead rope. I tried running past him a couple of times, kicking at his head as I went by, but he was still able to pull me off balance!

It seemed like days, but in reality was only a half an hour, before I realized the rope wasn't hurting me. When I finally stood still and let him flip that rope over my body and drag it back across a few times, he quit. Once again he went to rubbing my face, and scratching me in back of my ears. Then he started rubbing my neck and moving towards my body. He might be nice enough, but I wasn't going to trust *anyone* getting alongside my body. The last time I let that happen was when those two legger kids tried to kill me.

I spun around fast enough this time that I caught him off guard and got away. Dang near kicked his head off in the process. Lucky for him I just caught the brim of his hat!

Once again he didn't get upset like the other two leggers had. He calmly worked me into a corner, and when I turned around, he picked up the end of the lead rope. Once again we went through the routine with him flipping the rope over my body. After just a couple of minutes I was standing still.

He rewarded me with a little more petting on the neck, then started flipping the rope around my butt. I jumped and kicked out like I had been shocked with an electric prod! No Legs was able to get out of my way and I was more or less facing him. He kept it up for a few minutes, but all I could think of was being chased by that sleigh contraption again.

He switched tactics and went back to flipping the rope over my back for a few minutes, until I calmed down. Then he tied me to the fence and started to walk around me. When he got even with my withers, I started pulling back. I had to get *away* from him! He moved far enough back that I didn't feel threatened, and I stopped.

He walked up to my head and started rubbing me again. Once I was relaxed, he took a couple of steps back and started to walk around me. Once again I pulled back trying to get away. There was no *way* I was going to let another two legger put me into a predicament like I was with that sleigh!

About that time Grizzman came out and they started talking. No Legs asked him what he knew about my background. All he learned was where I had come from, but not about my experience playing reindeer. By that evening No Legs had checked around and learned about those kids playing Santa Claus and using me as a reindeer.

The next day he showed up riding a big steel blue mare named Sis. He tied her up, and then caught me. I was pretty easy to catch since I wanted to introduce myself to Sis.

The next thing I knew he was on top of her and flipping a rope over my butt. I started to turn and run, but halfway through the first stride I came to a sudden halt. It seems I was tied solid to the saddle on Sis's back and she wasn't letting me go anywhere!

No Legs kept flipping the rope over my butt until I quit trying to run off. It didn't take long because no matter what I did, Sis countered it and stopped me.

Next, No Legs built a loop and draped it over my butt so that it was touching both legs. I went to running and kicking, but this time Sis didn't try stopping me. Instead, she just kept enough pressure on my lead rope that I ran around her in a big circle. After a few laps around her the rope came off and I quit running. Of course No Legs just built another loop, draped it over my butt again. This time he was able to keep me from kicking it off. I was running and bucking around Sis as hard as I could. Neither Sis nor No Legs was getting excited; they just let me run around and buck.

After a while I got tired and quit bucking; a few more laps around Sis and I stopped and faced her. No Legs flipped the rope off and back on my rump a few times, then rode Sis around to my other side and draped the rope over my butt again. I flinched and took a few steps before stopping. Then they lead me around with the rope draped over my butt. It felt a little strange, and I kicked at it a few times, but I was realizing this wasn't hurting me.

Next he had Sis come up close to me and No Legs started rubbing me on both sides all over my back and rump. Once I was relaxed with this, he got off Sis and led me off to the side. He started flipping that long lead rope around my butt and over my body. I now realized he wasn't doing anything to hurt me and I stood there. When he moved alongside me, I shifted away from him, but didn't try to kick him. He brushed my back and under my belly. I did kick out at him when he started to brush my rump, but it was more of a warning.

Then he started sacking me out again with the old saddle blanket. When I managed to stand there while he did both sides, he turned me loose, got on Sis and rode away.

After a few days of being sacked out and learning to give to pressure rather than fighting it I was no longer afraid of things coming up in back of me. Within a couple of months I was packing Mrs. Grizzman across the desert and having a great time!

The Grizzman two leggers learned that while you can learn from a horse, that trying to learn *with* a horse is not a good idea. They also learned that it is a good idea to check the background of a horse, no matter how young it is. If they had known of the time I played "reindeer," they would not have tried to "learn with me." No Legs would have had a better idea of how I was going to react to things and would have brought Sis for my first lesson instead of volunteering to plow up my pen.

Monster

Give me a name like this and two leggers expect me to *not* have an attitude? Actually I didn't pick up that name until my second rider trained me into being a monster.

I was started under saddle by a horse trainer who sold me and a couple of other horses to a ranch in Northern Montana. I could do a fair stop, halfway decent turnaround, would pick up my leads and could open and close gates. All this was soon to be stripped from my memory banks.

I was placed into the string of a two legger named Sick, who'd been dubbed with the secondary moniker of WD-40® which was shortened down to WD.

Now WD was one of these guys who rammed and jammed on both cattle and horses. If the dust or mud weren't flying through the air you were going too slowly. He had no concept of giving a horse or cow time to think about what was wanted of them. Need to rope something and you'd better be moving fast enough to make a new National Rodeo Finals record. This was the man who would be teaching me the basics of being a ranch horse.

The ranch was just beginning to calve out two hundred first-calf heifers and fifteen hundred cows. This meant WD was going to start rammin' and jammin' on me with no basic training involved. Looked like I'd better be holding onto my feedbag!

I was initiated my first night. The job was to bring all of the cows who hadn't calved into the night lot, while leaving behind the ones who had calved during the day.

There was a cow trying to calve that didn't want to come into the night lot. As it was, her calf had a leg back and was going to need help. Ol' WD charged right at her trying to turn her, which of course didn't work. She was determined and I had never worked a cow. That didn't phase WD though. He started whipping, spurring, and jerking on me to catch up to the cow.

It was only by accident that I took off in the same general direction as the cow. When we caught up with her he started spurring me and jerking on my mouth so hard I didn't know if he was trying to turn me or rip my face off. Unluckily for me, the other two cowboys came down and relieved me of my duties so WD could "tune me up." It only got worse from there.

In only a couple of weeks, I started running off with him. After all, he was *always* wanting to go fast and *always* jerking on my mouth. Other than spurring me on both sides to speed me up, his only other cue was to reach up and spur me in the shoulder to get me to turn. His solution to my attitude was to put a bigger bit in my mouth and jerk even harder.

After four months of being tortured like this three and four times a week, I was a mental and physical wreck. I went from a horse who was willing to work and learn to one that had absolutely no desire to be around two leggers, let alone be willing to work with them. I had to be roped to be caught. Given the slightest chance I'd runway, I'd run WD under a low branch or slam his leg into a tree or fence every chance I got. I only wished I knew how to buck so I could plant him like a fence post! Luckily, after four months, WD quit and I was put into No Leg's string.

No legs wasn't particularly happy about having to ride me. He knew I wasn't a bad horse, but that it was going to take time to get the ghost of WD out of me. Our first ride proved him right.

He was used to horses in his string coming up to him to be caught, but of course he had to rope me. Once he got me saddled and a hackamore on me, we went out to move a small set of late-calving cows closer to the barn. On the way to the cattle he tried getting me to trot. I started to take off at a run, and he tipped my head around to the left, and dropped his left foot back to push my hindquarters over to the right.

Rather than pay attention to his cues and circling to the left, I started running sideways into the first tree I could find. He kept asking me to trot and I kept running off, then he would try to circle me and I'd find something else to run into. Half way out to the cows he decided it would be easier to just let me walk.

When we got to the cattle, we walked around them, and started them in the direction he wanted. Since I had been taught cattle needed to be pushed hard, I started running at the cattle. We were only moving them a half mile, but it was a half mile battle.

By the time we were back at the barn I was lathered up and No Legs was madder than Santa with an Elf Strike on Christmas Eve. What I didn't know, was that he wasn't mad at me, but at WD for making me into the horse I was.

Even though he didn't feel like doing it, when we got back to the pens, No Legs worked me some more. At a walk he would tip my nose in one direction or the other and apply pressure to my flank on the same side. It took a while, but I finally discovered that he wanted me to circle in the direction my nose was pointed. By the time I figured it out, my anger (and his) were over and I was strangely relaxed.

Gradually my anger and resentment began to fade. While it had only taken WD less than three months to turn me into a monster horse, it took No Legs nearly six months just to get me back to where I was when WD started riding me.

Once he had my trust, and I remembered the little things like turning, trotting and stopping, I made more progress. Rather than dreading cattle work, I was discovering how much fun it could be. My only two regrets were that I had ever been ridden by WD, and that it took so long to get over what he had done to me. Now the only ones who think I'm a monster are the cattle trying to run past me!

Miss Jekyll & Mrs Hyde

Up until I lost my second foal I was a total sweetheart of a mare. I'm a beautiful half Arabian mare, if I do say so myself, and I'm not the only one who thinks so. Several times I was placed in the top ten in both western pleasure and trail classes at the Arabian Nationals.

After I lost my foal, I was given a few months to recover before my two legger started riding me again. I really wasn't in the mood for it and made the ride as difficult as possible. Of course, my whole attitude was sour, but it was subtle enough she didn't notice it. After several rides I began trying to rub her off on the fences, reaching back and biting her foot, and crow-hopping. Since I was reminding my two-legger of the story of Dr. Jekyll & Mr, Hyde she took me to No Legs.

He decided to take me back to the basics, riding me in a simple ring snaffle. While I was still not happy about anything (let alone being ridden) his change to a softer bit helped. He also made me change directions quite a bit and practice lateral movements.

No Legs remained calm and didn't seem disturbed by my tantrums, which were getting smaller. After a few weeks, he made a report to my two legger. No Legs explained to her what I was doing, and how he was countering it. Even though No Legs thought I still had something bothering me, my two legger decided to take me home.

We more or less got along for the next few months, but only because I was trying really hard. Then my two legger left for college and didn't ride me for three months. When she came home and wanted to ride, rather than let her catch me, I kicked at her. Once again she took me to No Legs.

The first day he was to ride me, he came up to the stall, and I lunged at him as he opened the door. If I hadn't been lucky I would have bitten him. Even though I was cow kicking at him, and taking every opportunity I could find to bite him, he managed to get me saddled. While he led me out of the barn I squealed and jumped forward trying to get away. I didn't know what it was, but I was feeling like I was crawling out of my own skin.

Our first session left me really mad (OK, I started out mad, but I was even more so) and No Legs was somewhat confused. Come to think about it I was confused. I had always loved two leggers and now I couldn't stand them, or other horses.

Two weeks later, I still had the same attitude. No Legs was riding me in the arena and asked me to circle to the left. *That* was the last straw! I started bucking as hard as I could, swishing my tail and peeing all way across the arena. By the time I quit bucking, both No Legs and myself were covered in pee. After riding me a few minutes he put me away and called my two legger.

After discussing it with her a few minutes they came to the conclusion that my attitude problem began back when I lost my foal. This attitude was a highly amplified version of my "time of the month," and that hinted to them I was having a hormone imbalance. Since my two legger's father was a doctor, they filled a couple of syringes of hormones for an experiment.

The next morning, No Legs gave me a shot of the hormones and started working other horses. When he walked past my stall later in the day, I was back to my lovable self, and nickered to him as he went by. He came in the stall and I nuzzled him a bit while he just stood there scratching my neck and talking to me. I never looked a gift two legger in the mouth, so I didn't question how I was feeling, I was just enjoying the attention!

For the next five days I was one happy horse! No Legs rode me for two days and then had my two legger come over to see how I was doing, and go for a ride. Oh, what a happy reunion! When she saddled me up and rode me I was so happy and relaxed. There was not a thing she asked of me I wouldn't do.

Then on the sixth day, I felt myself slipping back into the rage. By the ninth day I was back into full blown "Mrs Hyde" mode. When No Legs came to my stall I lunged at him, teeth barred before he could even open the door. Not even bothering to open the door, No Legs headed for the house and brought back the other syringe of hormones.

When he came out the next morning, I was back to my old sweet self. Once again, I was little sweet Miss Jekyll for five days, before slipping back. By day number nine, I was back into full blown Mrs. Hyde mode.

Now that they knew what was wrong with me, I was taken to the veterinarian. It turned out I had an ovarian cyst that was making my body think I was going into heat. I had been in a state of PMS for nearly a year. Now that has been taken care of, and Mrs Hyde has not returned.

Rowdy

My name doesn't really fit me now, but at one time it did. I was never that big, but I was the baddest bronc you would ever swing a leg over. Of course, there were definite reasons for me being a psychopathic social misfit.

I began life as a mustang, running wild with my mother in the deserts of Utah. At three months old, we were run into a set of pens by a helicopter and separated. Within a couple of weeks I was run down an alley into a trailer and the door was shut. Several hours later the truck stopped and I was let out of the trailer into...*FREEDOM!*

Well, I wasn't quite as free as I thought. The pasture was only thirty-five hundred acres. There were no other horses, but for a few months a year there were several hundred cows over which I ruled. Other than the cattle, there were some elk and deer that followed my wishes. I was the king of my domain. The only time the two leggers showed up was to turn out cattle in the spring, gather them in the fall, and occasionally put out a little salt in between. When they were there, they stayed out of my way and left me alone. I was the king of my domain. Little did I know just how much things were to change.

The fourth time they brought the cattle in, three two leggers started chasing me around with some horses who were flat out traitors. After all, what horse in its right mind would let one of those two leggers strap a bunch of leather on their back and ride them around?

After several wild laps around the pasture I ducked into one of the pens and they shut the gate. After chasing me around in the main pen for another half hour, they managed to get me into a smaller pen with an alley.

They tried running me down the alley and into a trailer, but I managed to jump out of the alley. In fact, I managed to jump out of the alley three times before they got two ropes on me. Then they dragged me down the alley and into the trailer.

Several hours later the trailer stopped and backed up to a rickety round corral. I thought this was going to be an easy escape. The corral was low enough to jump, and the two rails were spaced far enough apart for me to crawl through. I was too busy checking out the new surroundings to notice the wire snaking into the trailer. The wire hooked the rope, which was fed over the top of the door and handed to the sawed off two legger standing in the round corral.

I figured I'd head straight across the pen (taking out the two legger in the middle) and just jump over the other side of the pen. The door swung open and I lunged out, teeth bared at the two legger in the middle of the pen. He stepped to the side just before I reached him, so I lashed out with a hind foot as I raced by. Then, just as I was gathering to jump the fence, the rope came tight and I was pulled off balance.

I wasn't pulled over, but just enough off balance that I turned, rather than jump the fence. Just who did this two legger think he *was*? It was obvious to me he had no idea of who I was, or that *I* was the one in *charge*.

When the rope came tight again, I reared up, but when I did the rope went slack. I was going to get *out* of this situation no matter what this sawed off two legger did. After four years of answering to no one but myself I wasn't going to start now!

I charged the two legger, but he managed to step out of the way at the last minute and the pressure was back on my neck before I could get gathered up to jump the fence. I charged him several more times, changing my angle of attack, but every time he managed to barely escape and had that danged pressure on my neck before I could reach the fence. Each time I reared up, the pressure would disappear. It was obvious this approach wasn't working.

I cut across the pen at an angle, but once again the pressure was back before I could get gathered up to jump. After several attempts I realized this wasn't working either and began running around the pen.

This two legger was baffling me. I had no idea why I was suddenly removed from my kingdom to be tortured like this, but I wasn't going to stand for it. There was a way out and I was going to find it!

I began running around the edge of the pen, trying to figure a way out. Other than keeping a light pressure on the rope and his focus on me, the two legger was doing nothing. After a while he suddenly made a move like he was going to step in front of me, and flipped the rope. I put on the brakes and wheeled around to get away from him. The two legger just stepped back into the middle of the round corral, keeping the light pressure around my neck with the rope.

I didn't know how I was going to get out of this predicament, but I intended to find a way. After changing directions several more times I was sweaty, tired and mad! I had no patience for anyone or anything. After all, I had just spent the last four years alone and was just fine with that!

However, it was beginning to dawn on me that the two legger wasn't chasing me. In fact, other than occasionally stepping out to cut me off, he really wasn't doing much of anything other than facing me. As tired as I was, I decided to stop, rest and contemplate the situation.

When I stopped and faced him, the rope around my neck instantly went slack. We both stood there, not moving, just staring at each other as I caught my breath. It wasn't just that I had no reason to trust the two leggers, I didn't even trust or want the companionship of other horses. After being separated from my mother four years ago, I had no social interaction with anything (unless, of course, it was to chase my subjects around for my own entertainment.)

After a few minutes of rest, the two legger took a step towards me. He wasn't being threatening, but I wanted to keep as much space between myself and him as possible, I turned and bolted off around the pen. I had figured out that if I kept my head bent in towards the two legger, the pressure wasn't as much. After a few more minutes of running around and changing directions, I stopped and faced him again.

Two legger immediately took a step towards me. I turned to run off, but he stepped in the same direction. I turned back and there he was again, only closer this time. By the time I decided to stop, he was only a few feet from me.

This was getting irritating! I couldn't seem to get away from him! All I wanted to do was get back to my kingdom and run free! I was the one who was supposed to be in charge. I didn't want a thing to do with these two leggers *or* the horses who allowed themselves to be ridden by them.

I decided to go back to my original strategy and charged the ignorant two legger. Once again he managed to get out of my way in the nick of time! The rope came tight again before I even got close to the edge of the pen. I turned and charged again, with the same result. After simply getting out of my way a few times, the two legger let me get closer to the fence before tightening the rope, and the next thing I knew I was once again loping around the edge of the round pen.

After several hours of this, I finally let him get to within a few feet of me. The two legger wasn't hurting me, I just had no intention of letting him touch me. I had been living independently too long to give in to what anyone, or anything wanted me to do.

The two legger started swinging the end of the rope at me, and I started to run, but the rope came tight immediately. I was too tired to put the effort into fighting the pressure. He flipped the rope at me again, and this time it gently touched a front leg. I struck at it, but didn't manage to get it.

The two legger kept flipping the rope at me, letting it lightly touch me all over my body. I started out trying to get away, but before long, realized I wasn't going to get away, and also that the rope wasn't hurting me. Finally I just stood and let him flip the rope all over my body, from both sides.

I was so tired I didn't notice him moving closer. When he started scratching my neck every muscle in my body tightened up, ready to make my escape. After a few minutes, he walked over and picked up a halter and lead rope hanging on the fence.

He came back and flipped the lead rope over my neck a few times, then started rubbing my neck, and running his hands up over the top of it. I was tensed up and ready for whatever came next. Then he started rubbing me with the halter. As he started to put it over my nose, I pulled back, grabbing the halter in my mouth and throwing it away.

The two legger didn't get excited, he just picked up the halter and started over. I was so tired I just wanted this day to be over with. After taking the halter away from him three more times, I let him put it on me. He went to rubbing and scratching my neck like he was proud of himself. I was only thinking "You're time is coming!"

A female two legger led an older saddled mare into the pen. She handed the reins to him and he swung into the saddle and rode to within a few feet of me. Taking a dally he backed the mare until the rope tightened on the halter. I braced myself against the pull and stood my ground. After a minute or so I decided I'd had enough! I charged the mare who somehow managed to duck in back of me and the rope came tight so hard it nearly jerked me off my feet.

I tried charging her a few more times, always with the same result. Finally I just braced myself against the rope. After a few minutes I weakened and took a step forward. *Finally* the pressure was off my head.

The mare started backing in a circle, taking the slack out of the rope and keeping it tight until I took a step forward. I was too tired to do anything else.

The yard lights were on by the time the female two legger opened the gate and let us out. I *finally* had my opening! I started to run off but the mare took off with me for a couple of strides before putting on the brakes. Once again, I nearly fell down from the sudden stop. Perhaps, for now, I would be better off to just follow the mare into the barn.

Once in the barn, I was put into a small space with high walls. The mare was led out and the two legger stayed in the stall with me. He rubbed my neck for a few minutes, and scratched me in back of my sweat-coated ears. As he walked off, I wondered how he took the halter off without me knowing. I also noticed a big pile of hay and bucket of water. I hated this place, but as long as there was food and water, I might as well eat. I'd be needing my strength tomorrow.

The next morning the two legger fed me before daylight. The other horses were nickering and sounding happy to see him. What was *wrong* with *them*? Didn't they know they could be running wild and free, being the masters of their own kingdoms?

A couple of hours later he came into the stall with the halter. I backed into a corner waiting for the worst. When he started to walk up to me, I charged, thinking I would smash him against the stall wall. Instead he stepped to the side and slapped my butt with the halter on my way by. The only thing I smashed into the wall was myself. Now I was mad and had a headache!

The two legger started flipping the lead rope all over my body again like he had done the day before. As much as I hated it, I felt my only choice was to let him do it. Maybe he'd take me outside and I'd get another, better chance to get away.

While riding that traitorous mare, he took me back out to the round pen. This time there were a couple of extra ropes, a saddle and blanket in the middle of the pen.

Once the female two legger led the mare out, No Legs started flipping the rope over me like he did the day before. Just checking, I tried getting away a couple of times, but as I thought, he just pulled my head around and I got nowhere.

Then he made a big loop and flipped it over me and stepped back. I made a couple of tentative steps forward and the next thing I knew the rope came tight around my body!

I gave a big jump forward and suddenly the rope around my body wasn't tight, but the one on my head was! I turned into the pressure and jumped again, hoping to land on him, but he was already out of the way! He pulled the rope tight around my body and I lunged again. Once again the rope around my body went slack and there was pressure on my head again, but not as much as last time. I began loping around the pen, just waiting for my chance to jump out.

The rope came tight again and I started to jump, but the rope was slack before I could get off the ground. He kept this up until I just kept loping without trying to jump. Then he kept increasing the pressure until I started to react, then instantly reduced the pressure. Once I quit reacting to the pressure he pulled the rope really tight and held the pressure constant. I really didn't know what he was trying to do, but I hated it, and I hated him for doing it. But he was making it impossible to do anything but what I was doing. After a while I got tired of pulling against the rope and gave in to the pressure. Once again the pressure went away.

The lessons went on day after day for a week. I tolerated being caught and led to the round pen. I tolerated being saddled and bridled. I hated every bit of it and took every opportunity to show it.

One day No Legs saddled me, put a snaffle in my mouth and tied the right rein back to the saddle. He didn't put a lot of pressure on it, and I had figured out that it made life easier to give to pressure rather than fight it. I stood there for a few minutes with my head to the side, and even took a few steps in that direction. No Legs walked up to me and I finally saw my chance!

I faced up to him and wouldn't let him get to my side. Finally he walked straight up to me and reached his hand out. I knew he was going to put his hand on my face...Not *this* time! I struck out with a front foot and caught him right in the belt buckle. As soon as he caught his breath, he came at me again. This time I caught him hard enough I tore the buckle off his belt.

He approached me again, more slowly this time, and circling. Once again I struck, but he wasn't there! I had a sharp pain on my lower lip and he had me by the rein...He beat me to the punch.

At the end of every session, he would go through the motions of trying to get on me. I didn't stand for this at all! I jumped sideways, turned my head and tried to bite him, and even managed to kick him in the belly a few times. Finally, after several weeks, he changed tactics.

He hobbled me and ran the lead rope between my front legs and around the saddle horn. I jumped as he started to put his foot in the stirrup. To my shock and surprise, my feet wound up next to my chin and I was lying on the ground. I wanted to kill this no-good, horse-hatin' two legger but I couldn't even get up off the ground.

After a couple of minutes he let me up and we started over, with the same results. Over and over he tried for several hours. I tried everything I could think of to keep him from putting a foot in the stirrup. Finally, tired of falling down, and just tired, I let him put his foot in the stirrup and stand in it. He rubbed me all up and down both sides of my neck and on my rump. All I could think of was, *your time is coming!*

The next few days we kept going through the routine. He would saddle me, drive me and then put his foot in the stirrup and pet me. Then one day, rather than just pet me, he swung a leg over me. He pulled my head around, he slapped me on the rump with the reins and kicked me. No matter what he did, I wouldn't move.

He called one of his two legger friends over. This one came into the pen, took hold of my lead rope and began leading me. I took a few tentative steps, and then started walking. This extra two legger stepped back and kept asking me to move out faster. After nearly an hour I finally broke into a trot. I even changed directions and stopped when No Legs wanted to, but I wouldn't go any faster than a trot...*His day is coming!*

The next day the extra two legger showed up again. After I was saddled and warmed up, No Legs stepped up on me and asked me to move. *Not on your life,* I thought. His two legger friend stepped into the pen with a rope and asked me to go forward. After a few laps in both directions, I broke into a trot. They kept this up for two hours, but there was *no way* I was going to go any faster. Finally No Legs got tired, decided he had other horses to work, and put me away.

The next day No Legs saddled me and warmed me up. Rather than thinking about how to get along with him, all I had been doing was trying to figure out how to escape, or at the very least, how to hurt him. He stepped up into the saddle, and before his off foot hit the stirrup I was loping around the pen. Strangely enough, he relaxed in the saddle... *FINALLY, here was my chance!*

I put on a burst of speed. He picked up on the reins to slow me down and I slammed on the breaks, rolled back and went to bucking. After a couple of laps he showed no signs of coming off. I changed direction and headed across the pen. Before I got all the way to the far side, I dropped my right shoulder and landed facing the opposite direction.

Another couple of jumps and I dropped my left shoulder and turned around in the opposite direction, planting No Legs on his head. *Got him!* Unfortunately he managed to get outside the pen before I made it back to finish the job.

After he caught his breath he came back in the pen like he thought he was going to catch me. I charged at him and finally knocked him to the ground. He rolled out underneath the fence, and came back in carrying a rope.

This time as I charged he swung the rope at me. I ducked to miss the rope, but took a swing at him with a back leg on my way by. *The fight was on and no way was this two legger coming out alive!*

I kept charging and missing him. Suddenly I felt the rope around my neck again. OK, he had me, but there was no way he was *ever* going to ride me again!

It took him nearly an hour, but he finally got a hold of my lead rope and took the rope off of my neck. He tried to come up to my side and I turned and kicked at him. For the past three and a half weeks I had been studying his every move. I was done messing around

Then the female two legger showed up on the old traitor mare and offered to lead me around the arena until I got settled down. She came into the round pen, dallied up and took me to the arena. I fought her all of the way.

Once in the arena I bit at the traitorous witch. I kicked her and sat back as hard as I could. Finally I managed to get a little slack and ducked under her neck. Within a few strides I managed to trip her up. We both went down but it was *worth it*

After checking to make sure the female two legger was OK, No Legs mounted the mare and worked me into a corner. I tried to blow by him but the rope went around my neck and came tight. The female two legger held the gate open and No Legs and the witch mare dragged me into a pen attached to the arena. After getting me up to the fence, No Legs flipped the lead rope around the top of a tall, thick post and stepped off the mare, letting the female two legger take the mare from the pen.

Now that I had him figured out, he didn't have a chance. As he removed the rope from the post, I charged him and managed to knock him down. But he didn't let go of the rope, and I wasn't able to drag him very far. He got up and I charged him again and somehow got tangled up in the lead rope, and down I went.

No Legs laid across my neck to keep me down, No Legs pulled the hobble rope off the saddle and hobbled my front feet together. Although I knew better than to try running in hobbles, that was the first thing I did when he let me up. When I hit the end of the lead rope I nearly fell, turned and charged him again.

No matter what he did or tried to do, I attacked him. He tried to reach out and touch me and I would either strike or bite at him. If he tried to touch me on the neck, or touch the saddle, I would cow kick at him. I was on a roll and there was *nothing* he could do about it.

I had to admit, he wasn't doing anything to hurt me. In fact, the way he was reaching for the saddle, he may have been trying to take the saddle off, but I didn't care. I was too mad about no longer being the ruler of my kingdom. The other thing I had to admit, he was *persistent*! The sun had been pretty high in the sky when I planted him on his head. Now the light was dim—the sun gone—and he wasn't weakening. Finally he got me next to the fence and wrapped the lead rope around a thick post, and reached out towards my nose. Once again I lunged, trying to bite him, and found myself tied with my nose touching the post.

No Legs went to the house and left me there to think. I was hot, tired and still really mad. I pulled back a couple of times and it accomplished nothing other than banging my nose on the post when I came forward. Now that I wasn't fighting with the two legger, I began to realize just how hungry and thirsty I was. As the night wore on, I just got hungrier and thirstier.

The sky was just starting to brighten from dark night when I heard the door open at the house. No Legs headed towards me in the moonlight. All I could think of was getting unsaddled and finally getting to eat. Surprisingly, I was actually happy to see him and nickered to him.

When he got to me, he scratched my neck and untied me. I gave him a friendly push with my nose and followed him to the barn. He unsaddled me and rubbed me down and turned me into my stall with plenty of hay and water. I ate, drank, and took a long nap.

When I woke up, I found myself thinking perhaps this two legger wasn't all that bad. I knew it wasn't worth fighting with him; I didn't want to spend another night like last night. I made the decision right there to cooperate with him. Within a few days we were exploring new places together and I was enjoying it. Perhaps being alone and having no direction wasn't all I thought it was.

Mare 237

I really had no problems. Stormy wanted me to tell my story because of the similarities between myself and Rowdy. The similarity was that we were both born and lived in environments with little, if any, human interference. The two biggest differences were that I had been bred for speed and quickness, and had lived with other horses so I *knew* what social interaction was.

I am a foundation Quarter Horse off of a large ranch in New Mexico. Until I was four I ran with a band of several hundred other horses in a sixty four thousand acre pasture. My mother weaned me naturally. Shortly afterward, the two leggers ran us into a set of pens and separated from our mothers and the studs. They then ran us through a chute and branded us with our identification number on our right hip, and the ranch brand on our left, then turned us out again until the next year.

The fourth time I was gathered, things took a big change. I was sorted off from the rest of the horses and ran down an alley, and into a stock trailer with a couple of other mares. We were unloaded several hours later into an old rickety set of pens.

For the next couple of weeks nothing happened. We had plenty of water and a two legger would come out a couple of times a day. Then one morning a sawed off two legger showed up in a battered old truck and trailer. He backed the trailer into the pen and put a couple of panels off the trailer door for a wing.

As he stood in the middle of the pen, I ran at full speed with the other two mares. Suddenly a rope snaked out and I turned to avoid it, finding myself in the makeshift alley, and then in the trailer. Before I could get turned around the door was shut.

An hour later I was unloaded into a round pen with solid sides so that I could not see out. A few minutes later the sawed off cowboy stepped into the middle of the pen, carrying a halter with a long lead. For the next few minutes he just stood in the middle of the pen as I raced around trying to get away from him. I had worked myself into a lather trying to get away before I realized he wasn't chasing me.

As I started to slow down, he flipped the lead rope in front of me. I turned like greased lightning and ran off in the opposite direction. By this time, he was turning and following me around the pen. After a few laps he backed off at an angle that would cut me off. I folded up like an accordion and shot off in the other direction like I had been shot out of a cannon.

He kept following me, making moves to change my direction with more frequency. Two things were slowly becoming clear to me. First this two legger wasn't angry, everything he did was calm and seemed to have some purpose. Secondly, he was acting an awfully like a lead mare disciplining an unruly yearling. Did he somehow understand this?

This second thought got me to wondering what this two legger wanted. Besides, I was getting tired running around and around with no way out. A few minutes later I lowered my head and started licking my lips. I didn't trust him, but, if my thinking was right, he'd quit chasing me.

It worked! As soon as I showed the horse sign language of submission, he backed off. He stood there, almost ignoring me, while casually flipping the end of the lead rope. After a few minutes he moved like he wanted me to move away from him so I did, but at a trot rather than a dead run. A few changes of direction and I started going through the submission routine again. Sure enough, he backed off a step, so I stopped and faced up to him.

This time he started flipping the lead rope in my direction. I'd turn to run but he would instantly move to turn me back towards where he had flipped the rope. Once again he put pressure on me just like a lead mare does when reprimanding an unruly member of the herd.

When we stopped the next time, he flipped the rope once again. When I started to turn, rather than just turning me back towards where the rope was, he backed off so that I stopped. He kept flipping the rope towards me and stopping my motion when I tried to get away from it.

After a few minutes, I stood to him, and he stopped as well, but just kept flipping the rope towards, me getting a little closer with each flip of the rope. When it got too close, I struck out with a front foot and pinned it to the ground... Instantly, the two legger came at me still acting like a horse that was disciplining another horse.

It only took a few laps before I gave the submission signs and he allowed me to stop and face him. He was still flipping the lead rope at me, but I knew it was wrong to strike it, so when it lightly touched me, I turned to get away. This time he let me go, but flipped the rope over my back so that it hung over me as I ran around the pen. I sped up and ran faster, trying to outrun the rope on my back.

The two legger just let me run for a lap, and then positioned himself so that I slowed down. After a couple of laps I realized that the rope wasn't hurting me and asked to stop. He let me stop, and I sniffed the rope. It didn't smell dangerous, so I waited to see what was next.

I barely flinched as he pulled the rope off of my back. He went to flipping it over my back and around my front legs. When he flipped it at my hindquarters, I kicked the rope before it reached me, and once again he moved me out. This time he kept flipping the rope at me, and in front of me. Once again, as soon as I realized the rope wasn't a threat, I began lowering my head, licking my lips, asking him if I could stop.

Once again he let me stop. To my surprise, I took a couple of steps towards him. He approached me slowly, with his hand out, and his palm up. When he got within a couple of feet, he stopped. While slowly moving his fingers he stepped back at an angle and I followed for a couple of steps, getting close enough to sniff his fingers. He smelled friendly with no hint of aggression.

He moved me out again for a few laps in each direction. His horse-like behavior was making me *want* to be next to him. The next time I stopped, I turned and walked up to the two legger. I sniffed his hand when he held it up and didn't try to run off when he started moving the back of his hand up and down the side of my face.

When he started walking backwards, I followed a few steps. He started rubbing the side of my face again, and I had to admit it felt good, sort of like being nuzzled by another horse. I stood there as he started rubbing my neck. I did spook a bit when his hand got close to my ears, and he moved me off once more. When I stopped this time, I walked up to him. He started rubbing me again, and this time I didn't spook as he put his hand over my neck. When he quit rubbing, he backed away, once more with his hand outstretched, palm up, beckoning me with his wiggling fingers. This time I followed him halfway around the pen. He stopped and started rubbing my neck again. This time he rubbed my nose, face and head. I was beginning to like this!

He sent me off again, but this time I was paying really close attention to him, trying to figure out what he wanted. He started asking me to change speed with his body position and attitude. Once again, he asked me to stop, and then beckoned me with his outstretched hand. This time I walked all the way up to him.

Once again he started rubbing me, but this time with the lead rope. I hardly even knew when he put the halter on me. He drove me out again, holding the rope on the halter, but letting it remain slack, with no pressure. After a couple of laps he took the slack out of the lead rope.

This pressure was a new thing, and I started to fight it. Almost as soon as I started to resist, the pressure was gone. He kept applying and releasing the pressure until I started giving to the pressure instead of fighting it. Once I gave to the pressure, he moved to stop me. Rather than beckoning me with his hand, he applied a very light pressure on the lead, which I gave to, following the rope all of the way to him.

Once again he rubbed and scratched my neck and face. Then, without warning he flipped the end of the lead over my back. I started to run off, but he put pressure on rope and I turned and faced him. However rather than wanting to come up to him I backed away. He started walking towards me fast, and working the rope so that I couldn't turn and run.

Once again, he stopped making me back as soon as I showed some signs of submission, and asked me to come forward. When I did, he rewarded me with the rubbing and scratching. Then he resumed flipping the rope at me. Shortly, I was standing still as he flipped the rope all over my body. At this point, he rubbed me once more, dropped the lead rope on the ground and left the pen.

He returned a few minutes later riding the horse called Storms. The two legger stepped off, picked up the lead rope and remounted.

After a few minutes of allowing me to get acquainted with Storms, and more practice giving to pressure, the two legger opened the gate and led me to my own private pen. It was a little cramped for my style, but there was plenty of food and water.

The next day we went back to the round corral for another lesson. Before this session was over, I was wearing a saddle and understanding that giving to pressure was a good thing. In less than a week, this two legger called No Legs was riding me.

A month later, No Legs went to work on the ranch he had picked me up from. I enjoyed the rides we took, and discovered how much fun it was to work cows. Since he had started out communicating to me the same way horses communicate with each other, I *wanted* to have a relationship with him. Because of this I learned what he wanted with no misgivings or battles. If Rowdy had known how to interact with other horses, he wouldn't have had such a hard time learning from No Legs.

What the author's friends say about him....

Leroy Garcia of Albuquerque, NM says; " _Greed and laziness are the parents of invention, Cowboys are the fathers of improvisation._" is one of Bob Kinford's favorite sayings that truly depicts his approach toward life. Whether it's a green colt he riding or a deaf dog helping him move 400 stocker calves through a series of gates with no other help, Bob finds a way to manage the situation and get the job done. He has a remarkable knack for working through the baggage that many horses carry and that other trainers have written off. When you see him ride with the romal reins swinging at a fast walk, the instantaneous blast from squeeze and planting that rear end in the ground on a loose rein, it's hard to believe that horse had any issues at all. You definitely can learn from Bob, I sure have.
(Friend since 1989)

Waldi Bloom of Billings, Montana says : "A hand, a friend and there for you when you need him, from can till can't. We rode together in Montana and Nebraska and I have real good memories for it. I'll never forget the time that "real calm" cow chased us both out of the barn, I scaled the gate as Bob ran down the ally with me yelling "Run Bob" and that rip blowin' snot up his back side. I've never seen anybody run that fast and jump a gate with that much agility!
(Friend since 1992)

Bonnie Mahl Gardnerville Nevada says: "Bob is like one of those colts that you are not sure if he will make the cut or not but ya keep him around because he has a LOT of try in him.
(Friend since 1977)

About the 2lazy4U Livestock & Literary Co.

Our brand is the 2lazy4U which looks like

Now as we all know, there is always a story behind every great brand, and the 2lazy4U Livestock & Literary Brand is no different!

I took a job in Nebraska to work with a man I'd worked with in Montana. Both he and his wife knew how hard old Stormy had been mashed on (just like all of the help on that place) and insisted he be turned into a pen with free choice hay to relax a few months before calving.

As mentioned, Stormy could be quite an exuberant handful when fresh and, despite my better judgment, I even gave him a ration of grain everyday knowing it would go to his head instead of his body.

The day came when it was time to sort the springing heifer s (ones which would be calving in the next two weeks) off the other heavies (pregnant) ones old Stormy became airborne. He was putting on quite a show bucking but staying with the cows, and turning with them even when he was four feet off the ground.

After about the fourth cow, my friend dryly commented "Bob, ya ought to grain that horse. He just doesn't have any energy."

I replied "He's too lazy for you to ride!" and the brand popped into my mind. (Come to find out both he and his wife had been giving him grain him as well!)

Other books by Bob Include:

Cowboy Romance (of horsesweat and hornflies)
This was Bob's first book. A collection of true stores from various ranches he has worked for around the west. *Western Horseman* said Bob "Mastered the genre" with this book!

A Million to One Odds (times five)
Livestock columnist and humorist **Lee Pitts** wrote the forward for this one and claims it is even better thn his first!

The Gourmet Cowboy (Cowboy style Gourmet cuisine)

Darrell Arnold of *Cowboy Magazine* said this is "One cookbook that belongs in every ranch kitchen!"

All of Bob's books, as well as information on horses and losw stress cattle handling are available at
                    www.2lazy4u.us

Made in the USA
Lexington, KY
13 December 2012